# Write Your
# Adventure Stories

Tish Farrell

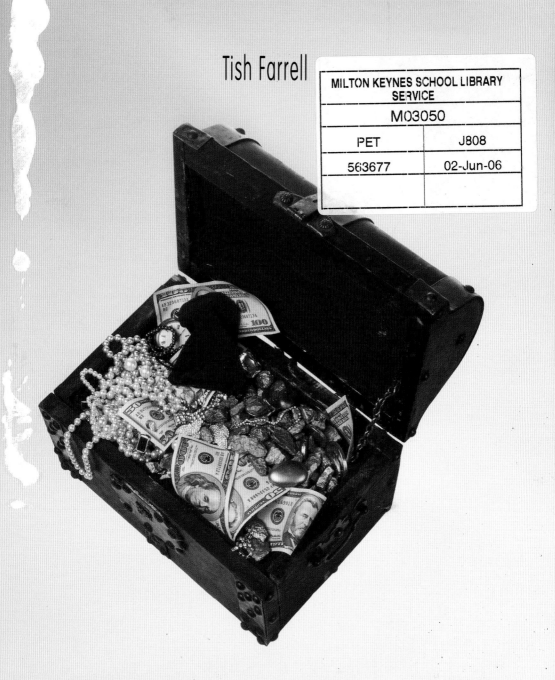

# Your writing quest

Do you long to scale Himalayan peaks or discover lost cities in steamy Amazon forests? Could you survive on a desert island, or drive a dog-sled across Arctic wastes? Now is your chance to find out. This book won't tell you where to find the Inca gold, but it will help you to write action-packed adventure stories.

Your mission is to blaze a trail to the Lost World of Imagination and find your own daring stories to tell. To help you on your way, there will be all kinds of brainstorming exercises and writer's tips that will develop your creative writing skills. There will be hints from famous writers and examples from their books to inspire you.

But don't forget! Becoming a good writer takes lots of time and practice. There are no short cuts to reach your goal.

Now, get ready for the big writing adventure...

# Good luck!

Copyright © ticktock Entertainment Ltd 2006
First published in Great Britain in 2006 by ticktock Media Ltd.,
Unit 2, Orchard Business Centre, North Farm Road, Tunbridge Wells, Kent, TN2 3XF
We would like to thank: thank Starry Dog Books Limited for their help with this book.
ISBN 1-86007-921-0
Printed in China
A CIP catalogue record for this book is available from the British Library.

# CONTENTS

How to Use This Book     4

## INTRODUCTION

Why do Writers Write?     6

## CHAPTER 1: Getting Started

First Things First     8
• *Writing materials* • *Writing places*
• *Writing zones*

The Writing Habit     10
• *Training* • *Brainstorming* • *Reward yourself*

The Reading Habit     12
• *Reading* • *Tastes* • *Look deep* • *Inspiration*

## CHAPTER 2: Writing styles and ideas

A Writer's Voice     14
• *Find your voice* • *Experiment*

Finding Ideas     16
• *Don't panic!* • *Freeing stories* • *Asking questions*
• *Ideas search* • *Real facts* • *Primary sources*
• *Computer games*

How to Create a Landscape     20
• *Invent a setting* • *Add detail* • *Location* • *Somewhere you know?*

Using Words to Create Worlds     22
• *Details* • *Recipe 1* • *Recipe 2* • *Recipe 3*
• *Recipe 4*

## CHAPTER 3: Creating Characters

Heroes     24
• *Names* • *Build a picture* • *A past* • *What's the problem?*

Villains     26
• *What kind of villain?* • *Motives*

The Supporting Cast     28
• *The cast* • *Revealing characters* • *Standing out*

## CHAPTER 4: Viewpoint

Who's Speaking?     30
• *The omniscient* • *Third person* • *First person*

## CHAPTER 5: Synopses and Plots

Ready to Write     32
• *Blurbs* • *Synopses* • *Story maps* • *Scenes* •
• *Inspiration from a classic* • *Novels* • *Short stories*

Good Beginnings     36
• *Great beginnings* • *Hooks*

Unmuddled Middles     38
• *False endings* • *Action* • *Weaknesses* • *Conflict*
• *The time factor*

Gripping Endings     40
• *Climaxes* • *Conclusions* • *Mixed emotions*

## CHAPTER 6: Winning Words

Making Words Work     42
• *Vivid imagery* • *Write with bite* • *Light relief*

## CHAPTER 7: Scintillating Speech

Creating Dialogue     44
• *Identity* • *Convention* • *Eavesdropping* • *Suspense*
• *Opinions* • *Different ways of speaking* • *Poetic speech*
• *Non-native English speakers*

## CHAPTER 8: Hints and Tips

Beating Writing Problems     50
• *Insecurities* • *Fresh ideas* • *Criticism* • *Inferiority complex*

More Tricks of the Trade     52
• *Beating writers block* • *Rebuild your characters*
• *Group stories* • *Journals*

## CHAPTER 9: Finishing touches

Preparing Your Work     54
• *Editing* • *Titles* • *Be professional* • *Make a book* • *Covers*

Reaching an Audience     56
• *Publishing* • *Writing clubs* • *Finding a publisher*
• *Writer's tip*

## CHAPTER 10: What Next?

When You've Finished Your Story     58
• *Sequels* • *A Famous example* • *Something new?*

Glossary/Find out more/Index     60

# WANT TO BE A WRITER?

**T**his book aims to give you the tools to write your own adventure fiction. Learn how to craft believable characters, perfect plots, and satisfying beginnings, middles and endings.

## Step-by-step instruction

The pages throughout the book include numbers providing step-by-step instructions or a series of options that will help you to master certain parts of the writing process. To create beginnings, middles and ends, for example, complete 18 simple steps.

## Chronological progress

You can follow your progress by using the bar located on the bottom of each page. The orange colour tells you how far along the story-writing process you have got. As the blocks are filled out, so your story will be gathering pace... Each section explains a key part of the writing process, teaching you how to get into the mindset of an author and learn all the necessary skills, from plot structure and viewpoints to adding belieavable dialogue. The process ends by looking at the next step - what do you want to do next after your story is finished?

---

## 16 FINDING IDEAS

### ❸ Dont panic!

The ideas for adventure stories are everywhere. You may find them in old photographs, newspaper articles or a museum display. Writers collect story snippets, and so do you – although you may not realise it. Locked away in your mind is a treasure trove of story ideas.

### ❹ Free your stories

When writers are planning a story, they sift through their ideas files. These could be notebooks, doodles or story fragments already written. They also sift through their memories. But if you are stuck for ideas, timed brainstorming is a good way to access your mental story files. By writing your first thoughts, you may set free some good ideas. Even if you do not spot them now, you may use them later.

**TIPS AND TECHNIQUES**

*Keep your brainstormed results in a special notebook or file. They may seem like nonsense now, but the next time you flick through, something may inspire you. You can brainstorm anywhere – when you are on the bus or even waiting for the dentist. Make lists – mental ones if you have no paper. 'How many words mean lost?' 'How many ways are there to describe a jungle?' 'Exotic place names.' 'Favourite heroes.' Exercises like this shake up your memories. Who knows what will pop out?*

**Case study**

*Michael Morpurgo bases all of his fiction on real life situations. He says: All my stories are based on truth of some sort, some nugget of reality. I need to have a face I recognise and put it in a book. I need to hear language. I need to have gone to the place about which I am writing.*

| GETTING STARTED | WRITING STYLES AND IDEAS | CREATING CHARACTERS | VIEWPOINT |

# Box features

Appearing throughout the book, these four different colour-coded box types help you with the writing process by providing inspiration, examples from other books, background details and hints and tips.

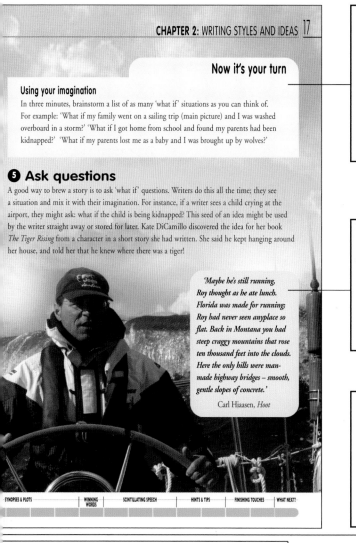

**CHAPTER 2:** WRITING STYLES AND IDEAS 17

## Now it's your turn

**Using your imagination**

In three minutes, brainstorm a list of as many 'what if' situations as you can think of. For example: 'What if my family went on a sailing trip (main picture) and I was washed overboard in a storm?' 'What if I got home from school and found my parents had been kidnapped?' 'What if my parents lost me as a baby and I was brought up by wolves?'

### ❺ Ask questions

A good way to brew a story is to ask 'what if' questions. Writers do this all the time; they see a situation and mix it with their imagination. For instance, if a writer sees a child crying at the airport, they might ask: what if the child is being kidnapped? This seed of an idea might be used by the writer straight away or stored for later. Kate DiCamillo discovered the idea for her book *The Tiger Rising* from a character in a short story she had written. She said he kept hanging around her house, and told her that he knew where there was a tiger!

*'Maybe he's still running, Roy thought as he ate lunch. Florida was made for running: Roy had never seen anyplace so flat. Back in Montana you had steep craggy mountains that rose ten thousand feet into the clouds. Here the only hills were man-made highway bridges – smooth, gentle slopes of concrete.'*

Carl Hiaasen, *Hoot*

SYNOPSES & PLOTS | WINNING WORDS | SCINTILLATING SPEECH | HINTS & TIPS | FINISHING TOUCHES | WHAT NEXT!

## Now it's your turn boxes

These boxes provide a chance for you to put into practise what you have just been reading about. Simple, useful and fun exercises to help you build your writing skills.

## Quote boxes

Turn to these green boxes to find quotes taken from published adventure books by popular adventure authors, from Sharon Creech to Michael Morpurgo.

## Tips and techniques boxes

These boxes provide writing tips that will help you when you get stuck, or provide added inspiration to get you to the next level.

## Case study boxes

These boxes provide history on famous fantasy writers - what inspired them, how they started and more details.

# WHY DO WRITERS WRITE?

**You can learn a lot by reading about famous writers' own writing adventures. Most will tell you that it took a long time before their stories were published. They will say, too, that it is often hard to earn a living as a writer. Here is some writers' advice.**

## David Almond

David had always wanted to be a writer. As a child he loved his local library and imagined his own books on the shelves. But it wasn't until he was much older and had been teaching for some years that he began to write.

He says: *Give your story a title from the very start, even if you know you'll change it. The title will help the story take on a life of its own.*

And: *Believe that you are becoming a good writer. Train yourself to find the good bits and to throw out or change the bad.*

## Margaret Mahy

Margaret sets her stories in her New Zealand homeland. She started writing when she was seven, but she was 33 and working as a librarian before she published her first stories. She knows it is rare for writers to have success with their first book. They all spend a lot of time working really hard and having their work rejected by publishers before they are published.

She says: *Know within yourself why certain books work well for you.*

## Sharon Creech

Sharon based her first young people's book, *Absolutely Normal Chaos*, on her own noisy family life in South Euclid, Ohio (she used her brothers' real names in the book). She used to teach English literature, and says that reading and talking about great books helped her to understand how to craft interesting stories.

## Lois Lowry (right)

*Read a lot. I mean really a LOT. And when you're reading think about how the author did things.*

## Michael Morpurgo

Michael used to be a teacher, but now he writes and runs a charity called *Farms for City Children Project*. He lives on a farm, and when he gets stuck with his writing, he walks around the fields telling himself (and his sheep!) the story out loud. He does a lot of research for each book, and a lot of dreaming. Then he writes up to six versions. He doesn't usually know how his story will end when he starts, but leaves it to his characters to sort out.

He says: *Write from the heart – as you feel your story; as you see it.*

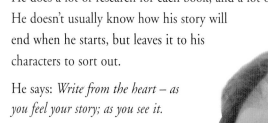

## FIRST THINGS FIRST

The first thing you need to do is gather your writing materials and set up your writing headquarters. As an adventure writer you won't even need to leave your desk to have exciting times. All you need is pen and paper to plot your gripping yarns, and perhaps a computer to write up the finished story.

## ❶ Gather your writing materials

You will need:

- A small notebook that you carry with you always.
- Lots of scrap paper and coloured pencils for drawing maps and plans.

- Post-it notes to keep track of vital information while you do your research.
- Stick-on stars for highlighting thoughts.
- Folders for stashing good story ideas.
- Dictionary, thesaurus, encyclopaedia and world atlas.

## ❷ Find a writing place

Finding a good place to write is very important. Your bedroom is probably the quietest place, and many famous writers do their best work in bedrooms, including Michael Morpurgo (author of *Kensuke's Kingdom*) and Morris Gleitzman (author of *Two Weeks With The Queen*). David Almond does a lot of work on trains. So have fun discovering where your very best writing place might be. Maybe the museum or Internet café have just the right atmosphere, but wherever you choose, remember to sit up straight while you are writing. Hunched-up work blocks the flow of oxygen to the brain, and adventure writers must be clear headed at all times.

## ❸ Create a writing zone

- Play music from faraway places to help you create exotic locations.

- Put up travel posters of tropical islands, rainforests, Inca cities.

- Wear an adventure-writing hat (think Indiana Jones). Make one or adapt one you already have.

- Choose special objects to have in your writing headquarters – an African carving, a mysterious Chinese box – anything to stir your spirit of adventure.

### TIPS AND TECHNIQUES

*Once you have chosen your writing space, the first rule of becoming a writer is to: Go there as often as possible and write! This is called the writer's golden rule, because until you are sitting at your desk with pen in hand, no writing can happen! It doesn't matter what you write – an email or a diary entry, even a shopping list – as long as you write something.*

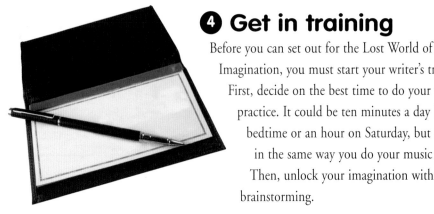

## ❹ Get in training

Before you can set out for the Lost World of Imagination, you must start your writer's training. First, decide on the best time to do your writing practice. It could be ten minutes a day before bedtime or an hour on Saturday, but stick to it, in the same way you do your music practice. Then, unlock your imagination with some timed brainstorming.

## ❺ Brainstorming

Brainstorming can be a great way to come up with ideas for your adventure stories. Ideas such as the ones below might be all you need to spark off ideas in your head:

• *You thought you were alone on the desert island, but one day when you went to the beach you found…*

• *You are the sole survivor in a crashed plane on a desolate mountain.*

Brainstorming with a friend can also be fun as everyone comes up with different angles on story ideas. No two people will ever approach a story in quite the same manner.

### TIPS AND TECHNIQUES

*Come stampeding elephants or plagues of locusts, make a date with your desk and stick to it.*

## Now it's your turn

### Free your creative thoughts

At practice time, have pen and scrap paper ready. Sit in your writing HQ, close your eyes and take four long, deep breaths to clear your mind. Now write 'Treasure Island' at the top of the page. For two minutes, write all the adventuring words and names that pop into your mind. Go, Go. Go! Don't think about it. Don't worry if it's nonsense. Flow like an erupting volcano!

## ❻ Reward yourself!

When you have finished the practice exercise above, give yourself a gold star. You are on your way to the Lost World of Imagination. The more you practise, the easier it will be to overcome the Story Spoiler or internal critic – the voice in your head that always picks fault with your writing.

## Case study

*Kate DiCamillo was inspired to write by reading the children's books in the bookshop where she worked. Every day she set her alarm for 4am so she could spend time writing before she went to work. Her hard work paid off when her first book,* **Because of Winn-Dixie,** *became an award-winning success.*

## ❼ Read, read, read!

All good writing starts with lots of good reading. Try to read as much as possible. Most adventures involve a quest, often in an exotic setting. The heroes must struggle against all sorts of hazards. Engaging, daring characters, like Mark Twain's Huckleberry Finn or Joan Aiken's Dido Twite, and plenty of exciting action are the keys to a good adventure.

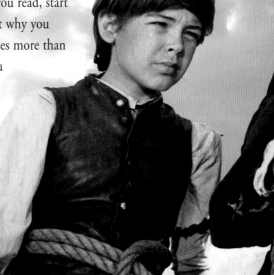

## ❽ Discover your tastes

The more you read, the easier it will be for you to decide what kind of stories you want to write. You could start with some classic adventures like Robert Louis Stevenson's *Treasure Island* or Jack London's *White Fang*. Or there are modern funny stories like Morris Gleitzman's *Two Weeks With The Queen*. Or how about Carl Hiaasen's fast-paced *Hoot*, a quest to save the breeding ground of some rare owls? As you read, start thinking about why you like some stories more than others. Do you prefer ripping yarns like the *Indiana Jones* films? Or do you prefer stories with a ring of truth? Keep a log of each book you read.

# ❾ Look more deeply

Go back to your favourite adventure story. When you first read it, you probably lost yourself in it completely, just as the writer intended. Now re-read it and ask yourself how the writer created such a believable and exciting story. This is another important step in learning to be a writer.

## Now it's your turn

### Operation brainstorm

Write 'Desert Island' in the middle of an empty page. Then spend two minutes writing around it all the thoughts that a desert island inspires – think of coral sands, rolling waves and scary forests. Do frightening things live there? Write your first thoughts.

## TIPS AND TECHNIQUES

*As you read, think about your own story. Do drawings of your characters and of lost treasures or cities. Read some ancient adventures, too. The legend of King Arthur might give you an idea for a modern version of the story.*

# A WRITER'S VOICE

**Y**ou've discovered that becoming a good writer means being a good reader. This is the only way to discover your own writer's voice – a style of writing that is uniquely yours. It is not something you learn quickly, which is why writing practice is so important. Writers go on developing their voices all their lives.

## ❶ Finding your voice

Once you start reading with a writer's mind, you will notice that writers have their own rhythm and range of language. For instance, Sharon Creech (author of *The Wanderer*) 'sounds' nothing like Michael Morpurgo.

## ❷ Experiment

Once you've found an author whose books you really enjoy, it's tempting to stick to them. Don't! Experiment. Once in a while read something quite different: a historical novel or a book of legends. You may be surprised what ideas it gives you.

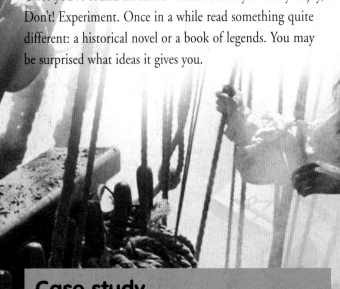

## Case study

*Geraldine McCaughrean started writing as a child, copying her older brother. She says she was very shy and timid, and the only place she dared to have exciting adventures was in her imagination, writing stories.*

# WRITERS' VOICES

**Look at the kinds of words these authors use.
Do they use lots of adjectives? Are they good ones?
What about the length of their sentences? Do some
styles seem old fashioned? Do you think this matters?**

## Robert Louis Stevenson

*The glare of the torch, lighting up the interior of the block-house, showed me the worst of my apprehensions realised. The pirates were in possession of the house and the stores; there was the cask of cognac, there was the pork and bread, as before; and, what tenfold increased my horror, not a sign of any prisoner.*

Robert Louis Stevenson, *Treasure Island*

## Celia Rees

*The deck swirled with smoke; it was like fighting in a fog. There was no time to draw a pistol, and guns are useless at close quarters. We had to slash our way back to our own ship.*

Celia Rees, *Pirates!*

## H. Rider Haggard

*On we tramped silently as shades through the night and in the heavy sand. The karoo bushes caught our feet and retarded us, and the sand worked into our veldschoens and Good's shooting-boots, so that every few miles we had to stop and empty them.*

H. Rider Haggard, *King Solomon's Mines*

## Sharon Creech

*We were racing along and it felt so terrific, all that wind! We had our foul-weather gear on, so we didn't mind the torrents of rain beating down as we ploughed through the water.*

Sharon Creech, *The Wanderer*

## ❸ Dont panic!

The ideas for adventure stories are everywhere. You may find them in old photographs, newspaper articles or a museum display. Writers collect story snippets, and so do you – although you may not realise it. Locked away in your mind is a treasure trove of story ideas.

## ❹ Free your stories

When writers are planning a story, they sift through their ideas files. These could be notebooks, doodles or story fragments already written. They also sift through their memories. But if you are stuck for ideas, timed brainstorming is a good way to access your mental story files. By writing your first thoughts, you may set free some good ideas. Even if you do not spot them now, you may use them later.

### TIPS AND TECHNIQUES

*Keep your brainstormed results in a special notebook or file. They may seem like nonsense now, but the next time you flick through, something may inspire you. You can brainstorm anywhere – when you are on the bus or even waiting for the dentist. Make lists – mental ones if you have no paper. 'How many words mean lost?' 'How many ways are there to describe a jungle?' 'Exotic place names.' 'Favourite heroes.' Exercises like this shake up your memories. Who knows what will pop out?*

## Case study

*Michael Morpurgo bases all of his fiction on real life situations. He says: All my stories are based on truth of some sort, some nugget of reality. I need to have a face I recognise and put it in a book. I need to hear language. I need to have gone to the place about which I am writing.*

## Now it's your turn

### Using your imagination

In three minutes, brainstorm a list of as many 'what if' situations as you can think of. For example: 'What if my family went on a sailing trip (main picture) and I was washed overboard in a storm?' 'What if I got home from school and found my parents had been kidnapped?' 'What if my parents lost me as a baby and I was brought up by wolves?'

## ❺ Ask questions

A good way to brew a story is to ask 'what if' questions. Writers do this all the time; they see a situation and mix it with their imagination. For instance, if a writer sees a child crying at the airport, they might ask: what if the child is being kidnapped? This seed of an idea might be used by the writer straight away or stored for later. Kate DiCamillo discovered the idea for her book *The Tiger Rising* from a character in a short story she had written. She said he kept hanging around her house, and told her that he knew where there was a tiger!

'Maybe he's still running,
Roy thought as he ate lunch.
Florida was made for running;
Roy had never seen anyplace so
flat. Back in Montana you had
steep craggy mountains that rose
ten thousand feet into the clouds.
Here the only hills were man-
made highway bridges – smooth,
gentle slopes of concrete.'

Carl Hiaasen, *Hoot*

## ❻ Real facts

Researching the background details for an adventure story can be like a history and geography assignment rolled into one. You don't have to know absolutely everything, but you need to know enough to see how the local details might affect your hero's story.

• Read *National Geographic* magazine and explorers' own accounts of their journeys.
• Watch documentaries about volcanoes and earthquakes.
• Search media websites like CNN and the BBC for exciting stories.

## ❼ Use primary sources

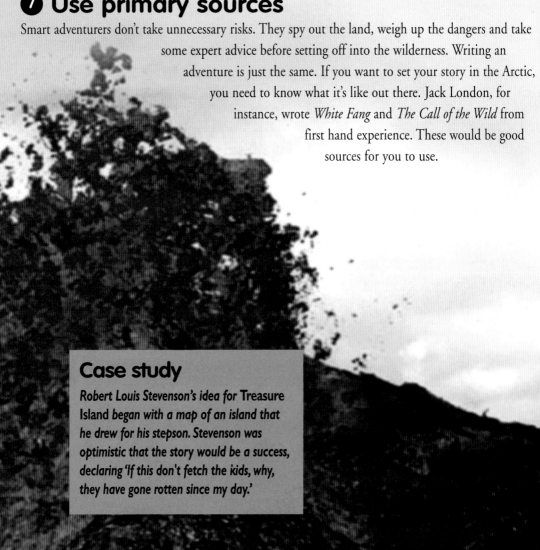

Smart adventurers don't take unnecessary risks. They spy out the land, weigh up the dangers and take some expert advice before setting off into the wilderness. Writing an adventure is just the same. If you want to set your story in the Arctic, you need to know what it's like out there. Jack London, for instance, wrote *White Fang* and *The Call of the Wild* from first hand experience. These would be good sources for you to use.

### Case study

*Robert Louis Stevenson's idea for Treasure Island began with a map of an island that he drew for his stepson. Stevenson was optimistic that the story would be a success, declaring 'If this don't fetch the kids, why, they have gone rotten since my day.'*

## Now it's your turn

### Getting a setting

Once your story ideas start simmering, you can help them along by describing the setting in detail. For ten minutes, brainstorm everything you know about the setting. Make notes under the headings 'Landscape', 'Vegetation', 'Wildlife' and 'Climate'. As you write, imagine being there. This will help bring your story to life.

## ❽ Use what you know

Holidays, school trips and outdoor pursuits will give you plenty of background material for a story. Keep a diary of all your experiences and record lots of details: colours, smells, sounds, how people behave, etc. Describe exactly how you feel, too. This is all part of your writer's training and could give you valuable raw material.

## ❾ Check out computer games

If you like computer games, you'll know all about the character 'histories' or back stories that brief you before you start a game. Games fans often discuss what makes a good game – interesting characters, plenty of action and an exciting climax – the same ingredients that writers need for their stories. Use some games ideas to help plot your own story.

### TIPS AND TECHNIQUES

*Story ideas can crop up anytime and anywhere. Always have a notebook handy so you can write them down as soon as possible.*

## ⑩ Invent a setting

In adventure stories, the natural world may have a big part to play when you devise your plot. It can provide a host of scary hazards for your heroes to tackle – charging elephants, sandstorms or volcanic eruptions. The more specific you can be, the more thrilling the scenes. Research carefully and be accurate with details.

## ⑪ Add detail

• To create exotic settings, use travel guidebooks for specific information.

• Study *National Geographic* location photographs. Imagine yourself stepping inside them and write down what it might feel like.

• Type your location into an Internet search engine. There may be travellers' photos and diary entries or exciting travel articles in the international press

• Read lots of fictional stories set in similar places.

## ⑫ A location's impact

In *Kensuke's Kingdom*, Michael Morpurgo only describes island details that dramatically affect the castaway, Michael. There are the shrieking gibbons that he hears when he first wakes on

### TIPS AND TECHNIQUES

When creating your setting, focus on details that will affect your characters and plot. Check your facts. Find out what an earthquake is really like or learn how a charging elephant really behaves before you include them.

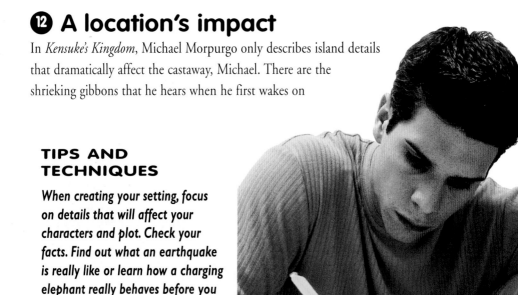

the island: *The howling became a fearful crescendo of screeching that died away in its own echoes.* Nightly mosquito attacks add to his sense of desperation: *From dusk onwards they searched me out, buzzed in on me and ate me alive. There was no hiding-place. My nights were one long torture, and in the morning I would scratch myself raw.*

## ⑬ Somewhere you know?

Your setting could be somewhere that you know well. If so, focus on things about it that will work well for your plot – as Carl Hiaasen does in *Hoot,* set in his home state of Florida. From the school bus, newcomer Roy sees a strange barefoot boy sprinting along the streets:

*'Maybe he's still running, Roy thought as he ate lunch. Florida was made for running; Roy had never seen anyplace so flat. Back in Montana you had steep craggy mountains that rose ten thousand feet into the clouds. Here the only hills were man-made highway bridges – smooth, gentle slopes of concrete.'*

Carl Hiaasen, *Hoot*

## Now it's your turn

### Tourist teaser

Look over the two sets of brainstormed notes about your exciting location. Now imagine you own some kind of wilderness camp there. You need more visitors to come. For 15 minutes, brainstorm a short tourist guide that you hope will attract them. When you have finished, start a new piece of paper. This time you are an angry tourist writing a letter of complaint to the camp manager. For 15 minutes, list all the horrible things that happened to you there. First thoughts only!

Read through both versions. Does the place seem real to you? Have you spotted some good hazards to use in your story? If so, it's time to think about how to describe them.

## ⑭ Picking details

Adventures are all about action, so too much description will slow the pace. Make the setting work for your story. In a jungle adventure, for example, you could show your heroes dripping in sweat or sidestepping snakes. Then drop them in a swamp!

## ⑮ Good setting recipe 1

Show the scene from a character's point of view. Here Jim Hawkins prepares to land on Treasure Island. His description suggests treasure and also a shivery sense of being stranded:

> *The whole anchorage had fallen into shadow – the last rays, I remember, falling through a glade of the wood, and shining bright as jewels, on the flowery mantle of the wreck. It began to be chill; the tide was rapidly fleeting seaward, the schooner settling more and more on her beam-ends.*
>
> Robert Louis Stevenson, *Treasure Island*

## ⑯ Good setting recipe 2

Combine description with a dramatic event:

> *Somewhere out there in the snow, screened from his sight by trees and thickets, Henry knew that the wolf-pack, One Ear and Bill were coming together. He heard a shot, then two shots in rapid succession, and he knew that Bill's ammunition was gone. Then he heard a great outcry of snarls and yelps. He recognised One Ear's yell of pain and terror, and he heard a wolf-cry that bespoke a stricken animal. And that was all. The snarls ceased. The yelping died away. Silence settled down again on the lonely land.*
>
> Jack London, *White Fang*

## ⑰ Good setting recipe 3

Trigger the senses. In *Pirates!* Nancy and Minerva escape to the Jamaican highlands:

> *We found a series of mist-filled ravines, with cloudy vapour escaping in ragged wisps, like steam from a lidded cauldron. We rode with our heads pressed to our horses necks, into dense dripping trees swathed with moss and hanging vines and spiky-leafed dangling plants that seemed to feed only on air.*
>
> Celia Rees, *Pirates!*

### Now it's your turn

#### Exciting openings

You may not have a complete story idea, but using your three sets of exciting location notes, write an opening scene of about 200 words. Combine sharp details of your location with some action. Maybe your hero is dodging a bear in the forest, or is being stalked by a gang across a demolition site. Or perhaps your story starts just as a huge wave washes your hero off a ship. Try to add some mystery or drama. What is your character feeling in your location?

### TIPS AND TECHNIQUES

*When using description in an adventure, say just enough to move the story forward. If you say too much, the story will sink like an overloaded canoe! Try to mesh the description with some action, as in the Pirates! example.*

# HEROES

**W**hen it comes to creating an adventure hero, there are plenty of models to choose from, from Robin Hood to Lara Croft. Whoever your hero is, you must care for them and show why.

## ❶ Find a good name

Give your hero the perfect name and they could spring into life. Make it snappy, with a certain style. Scan your dictionary, phone book or atlas for ideas. Now meet Beatrice Leep living up to her name:

> *It wasn't Mr Ryan who'd saved Roy from a whipping in the closet; it was Beatrice Leep. She had left Dana Matherson stripped down to his underpants and trussed to the flagpole in front of the administration building at Trace Middle School. There, Beatrice had "borrowed" a bicycle, forcefully installed Roy on the handlebars, and was now churning at a manic pace towards an unknown destination.*
>
> Carl Hiaasen, *Hoot*

## ❷ Build up a picture

What does your hero look like? Think about build, clothes and appearance. What are their likes and hates? Consider their strengths and, more importantly, their weaknesses. These could make your story much more dramatic, especially if they are scared of snakes, heights, small spaces, etc. Perfect heroes are just plain dull.

# ❸ Give your hero a past

Your hero had a life before the story began, and their history will affect how he or she acts. Sum it up briefly so it doesn't slow the story:

> *Kim was English. Though he was burned black as any native; though he spoke the vernacular by preference, and his mother-tongue in clipped uncertain sing-song; though he consorted on terms of equality with the small boys of the bazaar; Kim was white – a poor white of the very poorest.*
>
> Rudyard Kipling, *Kim*

# ❹ What's the problem?

All good stories are about heroes struggling to solve their problems. Adventurers are often misfits, too. For instance, Lila, in Philip Pullman's *The Firework-Maker's Daughter*, longs to be a firework maker like her father, but he won't reveal the final secret of his trade because she is a girl and he wants her to marry.

## Now it's your turn

### Creating characters

Take a large sheet of paper, leave a left-hand margin and divide the page into 36 boxes – six across the top and six down. Write these headings down the margin: • looks • always wears • always acts • is good at • is bad at • favourite things. Now take one minute to write in the top row of boxes the first six things you can think of about your hero's looks, e.g. scar on nose; lizard tattoo on wrist, etc. Repeat this for the other categories. You will soon know 36 things about your hero.

Now, for ten minutes, pour out your feelings about yourself: how did you feel when you won the race or climbed the mountain? How did you feel when you failed at the last hurdle or were dropped from the team – it's all raw material for your hero's strengths and weaknesses!

## ❺ What kind of villain?

All adventure stories need villains to challenge the heroes. These can
be natural 'enemies' like sea storms, breaking dams or great white sharks.
They can be human enemies. Or both. To add as much excitement as
possible, you need to show why these opponents are so dangerous.

## ❻ What's the motive?

If your story has a human villain, find out what makes them bad.
In treasure quests the villains are likely to be driven by greed. But the best villains
need more than one flaw to make them convincing. When you create your own
villains, don't be too obvious. Think sneaky, too. Perhaps your hero thinks the
villain is their friend.

Maybe they are very charming. If the
villain is a bully, remember there
are many sorts of bully, from
a tyrannical pirate leader to a
school thug. If an active
volcano is 'the villain of the
piece', build up the hazards
bit by bit; mirror the sense
of pressure inside the
cone before it blows. In
other words, give the
volcano a personality.

# Literary villains

### LONG JOHN SILVER

*Long John Silver seems like a goodie when Jim Hawkins first sees him at the Spy-Glass Tavern:*

> *His left leg was cut off close by the hip, and under his left shoulder he carried a crutch, which he managed with wonderful dexterity, hopping upon it like a bird. He was tall and strong, with a face as big as a ham – plain and pale, but intelligent and smiling.*
>
> Robert Louis Stevenson, *Treasure Island*

### BARTHOLOME THE BRAZILIAN

*In* Pirates!*, Bartholome is a buccaneer turned Jamaican plantation owner. When Nancy Kington meets him at her father's funeral, we know at once that he will become a serious threat to her:*

> *He took my hand. His long fingers were heavy with rings, square-cut rubies and emeralds. He stood looking down at me with eyes so black as to show no pupil. They held a gleam of red, almost purple, like overripe cherries, or deadly nightshade berries.*
>
> Celia Rees, *Pirates!*

### GAGOOL

*Gagool is the aged witchdoctor in service to wicked King Twala. She is set to kill Allan Quartermain and his friends:*

> *Nearer and nearer waltzed Gagool looking for the world like an animated crooked stick or comma, her horrid eyes gleaming and glowing with a most unholy lustre.'*
>
> H. Rider Haggard, *King Solomon's Mines*

## TIPS AND TECHNIQUES

**Villains will have weaknesses. In The Mummy, Benny's greed leaves him trapped fore City of the Dead. But don't forget: sometimes villains have good points too!**

## ❼ The rest of the cast

A dventurers – from Indiana Jones to Alex Rider – are often loners. But to develop them as rounded characters that readers want to read about, you must show how they behave with other people. This is why supporting characters are so important. They help to reveal the different sides of your hero, and they may also show the villain's true nature.

## ❽ Revealing characters

In *The Great Elephant Chase* by Gillian Cross, the hero Tad is treated like a halfwit, and even Tad believes this view of himself until the elephant (below) starts to change his ideas:

### TIPS AND TECHNIQUES

*Show – don't tell.* Instead of telling readers that your hero is kind-hearted, show them being kind-hearted in a scene with a minor character. In David Almond's Kit's Wilderness, we learn a lot about Kit by seeing how he behaves with his grandfather, whom he fears is dying. We see how much Kit loves him.

## Now it's your turn

### Standing out

Focus on your supporting characters. What are their special characteristics: their looks, the way they speak, their odd habits? Think how they could help or harm your hero. Imagine you are a team leader, recruiting members for an expedition. Interview the candidates. Look for those with the qualities you most need.

*[Tad] was being teased. There was no mistaking it ... Khush squirted again, with a perfect aim. Never hitting Tad's feet, but always close enough to make him jump away.*

*When Tad had been teased at school, it was always meant unkindly ... This game was gentle and amicable, and for a moment he was completely bewildered by it. Then, suddenly, he imagined how the two of them must look ... [and] started to laugh.*

Gillian Cross, *The Great Elephant Chase*

### ❾ Standing out

Minor characters won't be as developed as your hero and villain, but they must still seem 'real'.

A good way to bring them to life is to give them one or two obvious characteristics – like Mahbub Ali's bright-red beard in Rudyard Kipling's *Kim*.

# WHO'S SPEAKING?

**B**efore you start to write your story, you must decide whose point of view you want to show. Will you write from your hero's point of view, or do you want to describe everything that happens to all your characters? Do you want to write from the third person or first person perspective? The choice is yours...

## ❶ The omniscient

Traditional tales use the omniscient or all-seeing viewpoint. This way of writing tells readers all that is going on in a scene in a rather detached way, like a film-maker shooting a movie. The example below from Jack London's *White Fang* shows the use of this way of writing:

*A second cry arose, piercing the silence with needle-like shrillness. Both men located the sound. It was to the rear, somewhere in the snow expanse they had just traversed. A third and answering cry arose, also to the rear and to the left of the second cry.*

*"They're after us, Bill," said the man at the front. His voice sounded hoarse and unreal, and he had spoken with apparent effort.*

*"Meat is scarce," answered his comrade. "I ain't seen a rabbit sign for days."*

Jack London, *White Fang*

## Now it's your turn

### Good versus evil

Take 30 minutes to write a short action scene between your hero and villain. First write it from the omniscient or all-seeing viewpoint. Next write it from your hero's viewpoint and then from the villain's. Experiment with the first person and the present tense too. Read your efforts aloud to yourself. Which version do you prefer and why?

## ❷ The third person

Writing from only one character's point of view is called the third-person viewpoint. It is usually written in the past tense. It takes us right inside the character's head and involves us more closely. For example, the Jack London extract might go like this:

*Bill's heart leapt. A second cry! It pierced the silence with needle-like shrillness. He swung around to locate it. It's behind us, he thought, back on our trail. Then from the front of the sled he heard Henry mutter, his voice hoarse, "They're after us, Bill." Bill grunted, struggling to hide his own fear. "Meat is scarce," he said. "I ain't seen a rabbit for days."*

## ❸ The first person

The first-person viewpoint, that is 'I/we', is closest to the spoken word. It is intimate and exciting. Your characters will be revealing their innermost thoughts. You can use straight narrative, letters, emails or diary entries. The disadvantage is that you can only reveal other characters' views when recording their speech in dialogue or reporting on their behaviour.

## READY TO WRITE

As your story firms up in your mind, it's a good idea to describe it in two or three paragraphs. This is called a synopsis. An editor often likes to see a synopsis before accepting a story for publication. But don't give away the ending!

### ❶ Back cover inspiration

Study the 'blurbs' on the covers of some adventure stories. See how they say just enough about the hero and their problems to make the reader want to find out more. They also convey tone, showing whether the book is serious or humorous. Here is the witty blurb from Zizou Corder's *Lionboy*:

*Charlie Ashanti speaks Cat. He takes it for granted – but when his mum and dad go missing, the cats are the only friends he can turn to. Setting out to find his parents, Charlie stows away on an incredible circus ship bound for Paris. On board he meets six proud, beautiful lions who need his help. With danger close behind and uncertainty ahead, they embark together on the adventure of a lifetime.*

Zizou Corder, *Lion Boy*

# ❷ Create a synopsis

Before novelists start writing, they often list all their chapters, saying briefly what will happen in each episode. This is called a chapter synopsis, and it provides a writer with a skeleton plot which, like the general synopsis, helps keep the story on track during the writing process.

# ❸ Make a story map

By now you have created a setting, a cast of characters and a synopsis that says what your story is about. The next thing to do is to make a story map or storyboard to stop you from losing the plot. This is a very useful tool, a bit like that used by film makers to keep their movies in order during the production process.

## TIPS AND TECHNIQUES

*If you can't say what your story is about in a sentence or two, it is probably too complicated. Simplify it.*
*Ask yourself 'Whose story is this, and what is the best way to tell it?' Think about your theme, too. Adventure themes might be: proving your worth, overcoming hardship, courage, friendship, challenging evils or survival.*

## Now it's your turn

### Write your blurb

Try to sum up your story in a single striking sentence, then develop it into two or three short paragraphs. Think about your potential readers and look for ways to make them want to find out more.

### ❹ Split into scenes

Before film-makers start filming, they sketch out the main story episodes in a series of storyboards. This helps them to work out how best to shoot each scene. You can do this for your story. Draw the main story events in pictures and add a few notes to describe each scene.

### ❺ Get inspiration from a classic

Here are some storyboard captions for *King Solomon's Mines* by H. Rider Haggard.

1. Game-hunter Allan Quartermain agrees to guide Sir Henry Curtis to the fabled King Solomon's Mines to find his lost brother. Captain Good accompanies them.
2. A mysterious Zulu, Umbopa, joins their party.
3. Dangerous trek across desert and mountains to Kukuanaland, which is ruled by the wicked King Twala and his ancient, evil witchdoctor, Gagool.
4. Umbopa tells Quartermain that Twala usurped the throne by killing his father. Umbopa is really Ignosi, the true king.
5. Quartermain's party help Ignosi regain his rightful throne.
6. Ignosi spares Gagool so she can guide Quartermain to the mines to complete his quest.
7. Everyone trapped in the treasure chamber, Gagool crushed to death by secret rock door.
8. Escape through dark passages with only a few diamonds.
9. Say farewell to King Ignosi.
10. Discover Sir Henry's brother at an oasis on the trek home.

### ❻ Write a novel?

If you choose to write a novel, then a chapter synopsis will help you map out a more complex plot, and decide which characters you're likely to need to best tell your story. When you come to write, each chapter will thus unfold like a mini-story inside the larger story. It will have a beginning, middle and end, and carry the narrative forward by adding intriguing details and episodes that will entice and involve readers ever more deeply. In a novel there is much more room to develop your characters and much more scope for action scenes, and plot twists.

## ❼ Or a short story...

*King Solomon's Mines* is a novel, but it would work well as a short story. Mapping out the main scenes can help you write a short story too and keep you focused on the main character and on the most exciting events. Short stories usually have only one or two well-developed characters and a single story line, whereas novels may have many characters and several subplots besides the main story.

### TIPS AND TECHNIQUES

*Don't let a novel's length put you off writing one. If you use the storyboard approach, it's often easier to write a novel than it is to write a good short story.*

## Now it's your turn

### In a circle

If you are struggling to work out your storyboard, try this exercise:

1. At the top of a large piece of paper, sketch your hero or write their name.

2. Now ask them what their problems are. List the answers underneath and draw a circle around them.

3. Next ask your hero what they want or need to do to solve these problems. Write or draw these answers inside a circle at the bottom of the page.

4. Finally, ask your hero what people, places or things are stopping them from achieving their goal. Draw these in the middle of the page. As you do this, start asking how your hero means to overcome these obstacles; what will happen if they fail? What's at stake? Give yourself 20 minutes to do this exercise.

## ❽ Great beginnings

You have planned your plot and are ready to start telling your story. Your first task is to grab your readers' interest. How will you win them to your hero's cause?

## ❾ Hook your reader

Story beginnings have many important jobs to do – setting the scene, introducing the main characters, revealing their problems and conflicts and sending them on their way to resolve their difficulties. But where do you start the story? One way is to leap in at a crisis point. Alternatively you could play on a traditional story beginning, and mix it up to grab your reader's attention.

In *The Firework-Maker's Daughter*, Philip Pullman (left) humorously reworks a traditional fairytale beginning:

> *A thousand miles ago, in a country east of the jungle and south of the mountains, there lived a Firework Maker called Lalchand and his daughter Lila.*
>
> Philip Pullman, *The Firework-Maker's Daughter*

### TIPS AND TECHNIQUES

*When you have decided on the opening scene, start work on a mind-grabbing first sentence. For more ideas, use your library to study first sentences. Write down your favourites. Write and rewrite your own until you are absolutely happy with it.*

Draw the readers in by:

## Creating mystery

*Hassan. Where was he?*

*The question burned in Kibi's mind as he slammed the house door behind him and stepped into the village lane. It was a week or more since Kibi had last seen him.*

*Whenever he passed Hassan's house on the edge of the square it seemed shut up and sad.*

Tish Farrell, *Sea Running*

## Making characters intriguing

*I write for many reasons.*

*I write, not least to quiet my grief. I find that by reliving the adventures that I shared with Minerva, I can lessen the pain of our parting. I must find new diversions that fit my station now that I have put up my pistols and cutlass and have exchanged my breeches for a dress.*

Celia Rees, *Pirates!*

## Being funny

*The Queen looked out across the Mudford's living room and wished everyone a happy Christmas. Colin scowled. Easy for you, he thought. Bet you got what you wanted. Bet if you wanted a microscope you got a microscope. Bet your tree was covered with microscopes. Bet nobody gave you daggy school shoes for Christmas.*

Morris Gleitzman,
*Two Weeks With
The Queen*

## Being dramatic

*I disappeared on the night before my twelfth birthday. July 28 1988. Only now can I at last tell the whole extraordinary story, the true story. Kensuke made me promise that I would say nothing, nothing at all, until at least ten years had passed.*

Michael Morpurgo, *Kensuke's Kingdom*

## ⑩ False happy endings

Once you have caught your readers' interest, you must find ways to keep turning up the tension. You can create suspense with a false 'happy ending'. For a blissful moment the hero thinks they have won the day. But just when their guard is down, the problems come roaring back, bigger and bolder, and the challenge begins again.

## ⑪ Maintain the action

Keep your characters engaged with their quest, always on the move, working things out, coming to wrong conclusions, having fights or escaping disasters.

## ⑫ Add a subplot

In *Lionboy*, by Zizou Corder, the main story is about Charlie trying to find his kidnapped parents. Hot on their trail, he stows away on a circus ship, where he meets six lions. Able to speak their language, he promises to help them return to Africa. Now he has to find his parents and keep his promise to the lions.

# ⑬ Explore weaknesses

Don't forget your hero's weaknesses. If they are short tempered or rash, they might play straight into their enemy's hands, and reckless curiosity can land them in big trouble.

## ⑭ Add character conflict

Think hard about your supporting characters, too. They could add some drama. Are there simmering jealousies, acts of betrayal or simple misunderstandings that could make things tougher for the hero?

## ⑮ Add a time factor

In Gillian Cross's *The Great Elephant Chase*, Tad and Cissie are on the run with Khush the elephant from the dreadful Mr Jackson. They have to keep on the move, but how can they make an elephant go faster when his feet are sore?

## Now it's your turn

### Finding weaknesses

Focus on your hero's weaknesses. For five minutes, write your first thoughts on how these might complicate and add drama to your story. Perhaps your hero refuses to see some important truth; perhaps they are a bad judge of character and a friend turns out to have doubtful motives. Think how these factors might bring your story to a climax.

## 16 Dramatic climaxes

You'll need to bring your hero's problems to a dramatic climax. After this, conflicts will be resolved and the hero will return to a 'normal' life – having learned something important.

## 17 Write a satisfying conclusion

Most readers like some sort of happy ending but it is best to avoid the traditional story's 'they all lived happily ever after' approach. Your adventure story ending will need to be more realistic. Your hero has probably survived a tough situation and gained a lot in the process. They might have lost something too – perhaps a good friend. Or they might have had to learn a hard truth. In other words, they will be 'older and wiser'. *Sea Running,* by Tish Farrell, begins and ends with hero Kibi's thoughts about his friend Hassan. At the start, Kibi's blind admiration for Hassan gets him into trouble with some ruthless drug dealers. The story ends hopefully rather than happily with Kibi's realisation that *from now on, younger or not, it was he, Kibi, who was the leader.*

## Now it's your turn

### Excellent endings

Read the ending of your favourite adventure story. Are there other endings it could have had? Write one of them. Put it aside. Go back and read both versions later. Now which ending do you prefer and why?

## 18 Mixed emotions

The last lines of Anthony Horowitz's *Stormbreaker* have a dramatic, film-like quality. Alex Rider watches the man who killed his uncle depart. His feelings are very mixed. Alex has solved the mystery, but he has not found the justice he craves.

What other emotions does this ending evoke?

> *Behind the glass, [the assassin] raised his hand. A gesture of friendship? A salute? Alex raised his hand. The helicopter spun away. Alex stood where he was, watching it, until it had disappeared in the dying light.*
>
> Anthony Horowitz, *Stormbreaker*

### Bad endings

Bad endings are those that:

- Are too grim and leave the readers with no hope;
- Fail to show how the characters have changed;
- Fizzle out because you've run out of ideas.

### TIPS AND TECHNIQUES

*Good stories may seem to go in straight lines: beginning, middle and end, but they also go round in circles. The hero returns to the place where they started, but they are wiser now.*

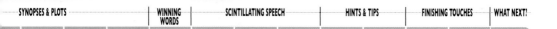

# MAKING WORDS

**W**ords are valuable things. Like water on a desert trek, you should use them sparingly and make every one count. In action-packed adventures, every word must work hard to carry the story forward.

## ➊ Use vivid imagery

Metaphors and similes are snapshot word pictures that help readers to see the scene swiftly. *In King Solomon's Mines*, Rider Haggard uses a metaphor to describe some giraffes *which galloped or rather sailed off*. In *Hoot*, Carl Hiaasen uses a simile, then a metaphor: *His legs felt like wet cement, and his lungs were on fire*. In *Two Weeks With The Queen*, by Morris Gleitzman, a comic scene is used to relieve a tragic mood. Colin has had some bad news and he defuses his anger and sorrow among the doctors' cars in the hospital parking lot:

*Ssssssssssssssssssss. Colin watched as the air hissed out of the tyre of the Mercedes... How dare they drive cars with automatic aerials and dual anti-lock braking systems and wipers on the headlamps when they couldn't even cure cancer?*

Morris Gleitzman,
*Two Weeks With The Queen*

## Now it's your turn

### Word workout

Give your vocabulary a workout. Brainstorm more lists: 30 adjectives and 30 nouns. Pair them randomly and see what you get: a blue-eyed boulder, a silken shield, a frozen feather. Reinvent famous sayings: as white as a crocodile's grin/as ice/as an Arctic winter. Read the dictionary, too, and play word games.

## ❷ Write with bite

When writing action scenes, choose words that 'sound' most like the action you are describing – 'smash' is more powerful than 'hit'; 'shriek' is more piercing than 'cry'. Vary the length of your sentences, too. Try short ones for fast actions and longer ones for more lingering events.

## ❸ Light relief

Adventure stories are full of striving and struggling, but now and then you need to give readers the chance to draw breath. Too much of anything can turn readers off. When they have had a break with some light relief, your return to your main mood (whether it is action or tragedy) will be much more effective.

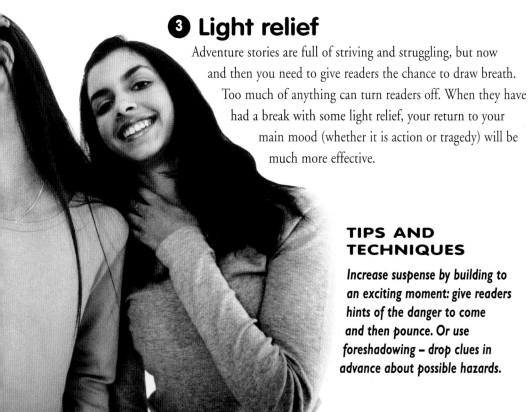

### TIPS AND TECHNIQUES

*Increase suspense by building to an exciting moment: give readers hints of the danger to come and then pounce. Or use foreshadowing – drop clues in advance about possible hazards.*

# CREATING DIALOGUE

**D**ialogue lets readers 'hear' your characters' own voices. It breaks up pages of solid print and gives readers' eyes a rest. When done well, dialogue can add colour, pace, mood and suspense to a story.

## ❶ Let your characters speak for themselves

The best way to learn about dialogue is to switch on your listening ear and eavesdrop. Listen to the way people phrase their sentences. Write down any good idioms. Did someone say 'I've got the hump', instead of 'I'm angry'? Watch people's body language when they are whispering or arguing. LOOK, LISTEN, ABSORB!

## Now it's your turn

### Standing out

Tune in to a TV chat show. Spend ten minutes writing down exactly what people say, including all the 'ums', 'ers' and repetitions. Listen out for a range of voices: young, old, with a different education or from a different community. Next compare it with some dialogue in a book. You will see at once that written dialogue does not include all the hesitations of natural speech, but gives an edited impression of how people speak.

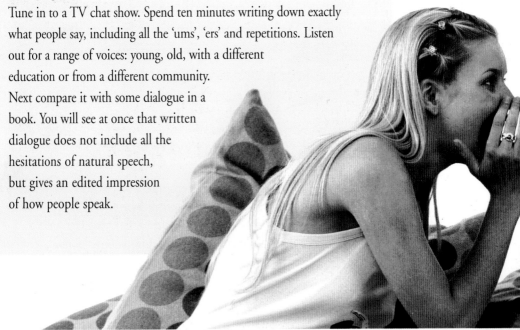

# ❷ Following convention

The way dialogue is written follows certain conventions or rules. It is usual to start a new paragraph for every new speaker. What they say is enclosed in single or double inverted commas, followed by speech tags – "he said/she said". Putting the speech tags in the middle of a line can give a sense of real conversation, as in this extract from *Stormbreaker* by Anthony Horowitz.

> *'My name is Alan Blunt,' he said. 'Your uncle often spoke of you.'*
> *'That's funny,' Alex said. 'He never mentioned you.'*
> *The grey lips twitched briefly. 'We'll miss him. He was a good man.'*
> *'What was he good at?' Alex asked. 'He never talked about his work.'*
> *Suddenly Crawley was there. 'Your uncle was Overseas Finance Manager, Alex,' he said.*
> *'He was responsible for all our foreign branches. You must have known that?'*
>
> Anthony Horowitz, *Stormbreaker*

## TIPS AND TECHNIQUES

*When writing dialogue, don't just stick to 'he said/she said' all the time. Use words like 'asked', 'replied' 'exclaimed', 'cried', 'whispered', etc. to create excitement and variety in your writing.*

### ❸ Fictional eavesdropping

Details about a place or character can often be told much more quickly in a conversation. This is a good way to move the story on.

### ❹ Create suspense

A scene can be written more humorously or dramatically in a series of spoken exchanges. In *Hoot*, Roy trails the running boy to his hideout, but when he opens a rubbish sack he finds himself in danger:

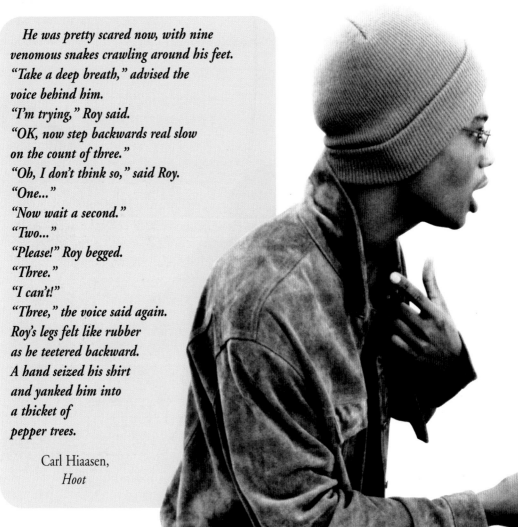

*He was pretty scared now, with nine venomous snakes crawling around his feet.*
*"Take a deep breath," advised the voice behind him.*
*"I'm trying," Roy said.*
*"OK, now step backwards real slow on the count of three."*
*"Oh, I don't think so," said Roy.*
*"One..."*
*"Now wait a second."*
*"Two..."*
*"Please!" Roy begged.*
*"Three."*
*"I can't!"*
*"Three," the voice said again.*
*Roy's legs felt like rubber as he teetered backward.*
*A hand seized his shirt and yanked him into a thicket of pepper trees.*

Carl Hiaasen,
*Hoot*

## Now it's your turn

### Crafting a conversation

Think of a scene where an explanation is needed – perhaps to account for your hero's behaviour. Write it first as a piece of narrative to get down all the details. Then convey the same information as a conversation. Try to make the characters sound different from each other.

## ❺ Give character's viewpoints and opinions

If you are telling the story from your hero's viewpoint, dialogue is the only way for readers to hear directly from the other characters. In *The Kite Rider* by Geraldine McCaughrean, the story is told from Haoyou's viewpoint. In the next extract, greedy Great-Uncle Bo has tracked him down and demands all his nephew's circus earnings:

### TIPS AND TECHNIQUES

*Dialogue can add drama if the characters lie. It can also be used to drop hints about dangers that lie ahead.*

"Where's the money?"
"What money?"
"The gold the Khan gave you!"
"But – I was going to send it to my mother and Wawa!"
"Nonsense. I can put it to good use. I've made a wager."
He took Haoyou's hair and coaxed him out of the tent by it. Encouraged by Miao Jie's earlier talk of defiance, Haoyou dared to persist: "I want to send it home to Mother. It's special. From Tibet! I want her to see it!"
"Gold's gold," said Bo...
"Now do as you are told."

Geraldine McCaughrean,
*The Kite Rider*

# Find different ways of speaking

In the last exercise you practised creating different speakers. If you found it hard, don't worry – it is the most difficult thing for a writer to do. Even well-known writers aren't always good at writing dialogue. Remember, your characters won't necessarily speak like you.

## ❼ Poetic speech

Curly, in Carl Hiaasen's *Hoot*, is the angry construction site foreman. He thinks he's caught Roy sabotaging the site. See how Hiaasen suggests that Curly isn't very well educated:

> *"What's your name? What're you doing here?" the foreman hollered.*
> *"This is private property, don't you know that? You wanna go to jail, junior?"*
> *Roy stopped pedalling and caught his breath.*
> *"I know what you're up to!" the bald man snarled. "I know your sneaky game."*
> *Roy said, "Please, mister, let me go. I was only feeding the owls."*
> *The crimson drained from the foreman's cheeks.*
> *"What owls?" he said, not so loudly. "There ain't no owls around here."*
> *"Oh, yes, there are," Roy said. "I've seen them."*
> *The bald guy looked extremely nervous and agitated... "Listen to me, boy.*
> *You didn't see no damn owls, OK? What you*
> *saw was a wild chicken!"*
>
> Carl Hiaasen, *Hoot*

## TIPS AND TECHNIQUES

If your character has a foreign accent, don't attempt to replicate it exactly. Instead, find w to suggest the accent only – either in the way the speech is phrased, or the occasional use dialect or foreign word, such as a greeting.

## ❽ Non-native English speaker

Kensuke is doctor who has been stranded on a desert island since the Second World War. Notice the respectful Japanese 'san' attached to the end of Kensuke's version of Michael's name. Also, the views he expresses are characteristic of oriental philosophy:

> *"It is easier when you are old like me, Micasan," he said. "What is?" I asked. "Waiting," he said. "One day a ship will come, Micasan. Maybe soon, maybe not so soon. But it will come. Life must not be spent always hoping, always waiting. Life is for living."*
>
> Michael Morpurgo,
> *Kensuke's Kingdom*

## ❾ Use accents

Allie Keenan's north-east England accent is suggested by the rhythm of her words, and the use of 'man' after Kit's name. She has a catchphrase too: 'Drive me wild'. Here she 'rescues' Kit from Askew's *Death Game*:

> *"Come on," she said. "Pull yourself together." I took long deep breaths, shook my head, tried to smile at her. "You," she said. "Too innocent, that's your trouble. Drive me wild." She squeezed my arm. We walked on. She took me towards the gate. "Kit," she kept saying. "Kit, man. Kit." I looked again across the wilderness. "Do you see them?" I whispered. "See? See what?" She stared into my eyes. "Kit, man. See what?"*
>
> David Almond, *Kit's Wilderness*

## Now it's your turn

### Generation gap

Write down a conversation between you and one of your parents. Try to capture exactly how they speak. What words or phrases do they always use that are different from yours? What expressions do you always use? When you have finished, rewrite the conversation, replacing one of the characters with a grandparent or older person. Are there more differences?

# BEATING WRITER'S BLOCK

Even the most dogged adventurers run out of steam, and so can writers. They run out of words or the will to write. This is called writer's block. It can last for days or sometimes even longer. Here are some of the causes and how to overcome them.

## ❶ Get over your insecurities

Back on page 11, I mentioned the Story Spoiler – your internal critic that picks faults with everything you write and eventually drives you back to the TV. Do not listen! Brainstorm something positive immediately – how it felt to score the winning point. Think Indiana Jones! Show the Story Spoiler your bullwhip!

## ❷ Find fresh ideas

Having nothing to say is a common excuse that writers give for not writing. But if you have been doing your writing practice regularly and following the exercises, you will always find something to say. It doesn't matter how good or clever it is, just write it down. You will learn to write even when you don't feel inspired. Don't forget! Ideas are everywhere.

# ❸ Handle criticism

No one enjoys rejection or criticism, but learning to accept them is an important part of becoming a writer. If you ask someone to read your work, be prepared for negative comments. See both fair criticism and rejection as opportunities to rewrite your story.

# ❹ Don't assume other writers are better than you

This thought is guaranteed to give you writer's block, so again – show it your bullwhip! How good a writer you become is up to you and how hard you work at it. Only *you* can tell your stories, and just because you might not succeed as a fiction writer, doesn't mean that you won't be a top journalist.

## Now it's your turn

### Prove it!

Prove to yourself you can write right now. Watch your favourite TV or film adventure. Rewrite your own version of the story. Change the characters or turn a minor character into the hero. Taking notes on how well TV stories work can teach you a lot about constructing a gripping narrative.

## ❺ Don't get marooned!

The loneliness of being a writer can often stop people writing. So if you start feeling marooned, call in some friends to try out your story ideas on. Sit in a circle and tell your friends your story so far. Put on the skin of your hero and let your friends interrogate you. Who are you? What do you really want? What is at stake? What or who is stopping you from solving your problems? What can you do about this? They could ask you about your history too – where you came from or how you got lost.

## ❻ Build your character again

Group brainstorming can help bring your character to life. Start by writing a brief character description at the top of a sheet of paper. After two minutes, pass it to a friend to add their ideas. When two minutes are up, the next person develops the description. Mull over the results. Have you learned anything new about your character?

# ❼ Make a group story

First cut up some scrap paper into 36 squares. Choose someone to do the writing. Then go around the circle and brainstorm 12 character ideas – perhaps a big-game hunter. Next brainstorm 12 objects – maybe a Zanzibari treasure chest. Finally brainstorm 12 locations – perhaps the Great Wall of China! Shuffle the three piles and place them face down in the middle. Everyone should choose one card and take turns to weave their character, place or object into the story. The end result will be something like a chapter synopsis. Another option is to get everyone to pick a sentence from their favourite adventure story. All the choices must be worked into a group story.

## TIPS AND TECHNIQUES

*When you are stuck for words, going for a walk can inspire ideas. Or try looking under your bed. Everything you threw there months ago will have a memory attached. It could be just the clue you need to restart your story. Sometimes a stalled story simply needs to brew for a while. Start something new while you wait.*

# ❽ Keep a journal

Many adventure stories are written as diary entries, so keeping your own diary is useful. It also helps prevent writer's block. Set yourself a daily target, say 300 words. See how you can turn the day's events into an anecdote or dramatic story. And definitely record all holiday travels.

# PREPARING YOUR WORK

**W**hen your first story has been 'resting' in your desk drawer for a month, take it out and do some revision. You will be able to read it with fresh eyes and it will be easier to spot any flaws.

## ❶ Editing

Reading your work aloud will help you to simplify rambling sentences and correct dialogue that doesn't flow. Cut out all unnecessary adjectives and adverbs and words like 'very'. This will instantly make your writing crisper. Think about the story, too. Does it have a satisfying end? Has the hero resolved their problem in the best way? Does the end link with the beginning, and has your hero learned something and changed? When your story is as good as can be, write it out afresh or type it up on a computer. This is your manuscript.

## ❷ Think of a title

It is important to think up a good title; choose something intriguing and eye-catching. Think about some titles you know and like.

## ❸ Be professional

If you are sending your manuscript to a publisher, magazine or agent, it's best to type it up. Manuscripts should always be printed on one side of A4 white paper, with wide margins and double line spacing. Pages should be numbered and new chapters should start on a new page. You can include your title as a header on the top of each page. At the front, have a title page that gives your name, address, telephone number and email address.

# ❹ Make your own book

If your school has its own publishing lab, why not use it to 'publish' your own story or make a class story anthology (collection). A computer will let you choose your own font (print style) or justify the text (making even length margins like a professionally printed page). When you have typed and saved your story to a file, you can edit it quickly with the spell- and grammar checker, or move sections of your story

around using the 'cut and paste' facility, which saves a lot of rewriting. Having your story on a computer file also means you can print a copy whenever you need one, or revise the whole story if you want to.

# ❺ Design a cover

Once your story is in good shape, you can print it out and then use the computer to design the cover. A graphics program will let you scan and print your own artwork, or download ready-made graphics. Or you could use your own digital photographs and learn how to manipulate them on screen to produce some highly original images. You can use yourself or friends as 'models' for your story's heroes.

## TIPS AND TECHNIQUES

*Whether you write your story on a computer or by hand, always make a copy before you give it to anyone else to read. If they lose it, you will have lost all your precious work!*

## ❻ Some places to publish your story

The next step is to find an audience for your adventure-fiction work. Family members or classmates may be receptive. Or you may want to get your work published via a publishing house or online site. There are several magazines and a number of writing websites that accept stories and novel chapters from young adventure-fiction writers. Some give writing advice. Several run regular competitions. Each site has its own rules about submitting work to them, so make sure you read them carefully before you send in a story. See page 62 for more details. You can also:

- Send stories to your school magazine.
  If your school doesn't have a magazine, start your own with like-minded friends!

- Keep your eyes peeled when reading your local newspaper or magazines. They might be running a writing competition you could enter.

- Check with local museums and colleges. Some run creative-writing workshops during school holidays.

## ❼ Writing clubs

Starting a writing club or critique group and exchanging stories is a great way of getting your adventure-fiction story out there. It will also get you used to criticism from others, which will prove invaluable in learning how to write. Your local library might be kind enough to provide a forum for such a club.

## ❽ Finding a publisher

Secure any submission with a paperclip and always enclose a short letter (saying what you have sent) and a stamped, addressed envelope for the story's return. Study the market and find out which publishing houses are most likely to publish adventure stories. Addresses of publishing houses and

information about whether they accept submissions can be found in writers' handbooks. Bear in mind that manuscripts that haven't been asked for or paid for by a publisher – unsolicited submissions – are rarely published.

## ⑨ Writer's tip

If your story is rejected by an editor, don't despair! See it as a chance to make the story better and try again. And remember; having your work published is wonderful, but it is not the only thing. Being able to make up stories is a gift, so why not give yours to someone you love? Read it to a younger brother or sister. Tell it to your grandfather.

Find your audience!

### TIPS AND TECHNIQUES

*READ, READ, READ, WRITE, WRITE, WRITE. Head for the next big adventure!*

## Case study

*David Almond spent five years writing an adult novel that was rejected by every publisher. Then he had the idea of a filthy, irritable, arthritic man living off live spiders in a derelict garage, and he began the story of the mysterious winged being, Skellig. It became a major bestseller. Writers can try too hard to write for the wrong audience!*

# WHEN YOU'VE FINISHED YOUR STORY

**W**ell done! Finishing your first story is a stunning achievement! You have reached the Lost World of Imagination and created something entirely new. You have proved you can write and probably learned a lot about yourself too. But now it's time to set out on a new adventure and start a new story.

## ❶ How about a sequel?

When thinking about your next work, ask yourself: 'Do I want to send the characters I created on another adventure? Is there more to tell about them in a sequel to my first story?' Occasionally, adventure stories are written as trilogies, like *Lion Boy* by Zizou Corder. The three-book structure mimics the beginning, middle and end of all stories: book one starts the adventure; book two fattens and complicates the story; and book three brings the story to a climax and a satisfying conclusion.

## ❷ A famous example

Sometimes a hero is so intriguing and pushy that they demand more tales about them. Joan Aiken's Dido Twite is just such a character. This brave,

## Now it's your turn

### New challenges

To see if your hero is ready for a new adventure, try this exercise. Take a large sheet of paper and at the centre draw your main character inside a circle. Then draw six lines radiating out to six more circles. Now imagine you are the hero looking around for a new challenge. Ask yourself: 'What is my new problem?' 'Where am I going next?' For ten minutes brainstorm your first thoughts, putting one idea in each of the circles. If some of your results seem totally mad, don't worry. You may find that, with a little more thought, they are good ideas after all.

smart-talking, smart-thinking Cockney waif first appeared in *Black Hearts in Battersea* (a sequel to *The Wolves of Willoughby Chase*), only to be lost at sea at the end of the book. But in *Nightbirds in Nantucket* she comes sailing back aboard Captain Coffin's whaler and is soon set to foil another wicked Hanoverian plot.

### ❸ Something new

Perhaps while you were writing the first story, some new ideas cropped up and you made a note of them in your 'ideas file'. Take them out. Do they still excite you? If so, go back to the start of this book and repeat some of the brainstorming exercises to help you develop the ideas further. This time round you already know you can write a story.

**back story** – the history of people or events that happened before the actual story begins

**chapter synopsis** – an outline description saying briefly what is to happen in each chapter

**cliffhanger** – a nail-biting moment at the end of a chapter or just as the writer switches viewpoints

**dramatic irony** – the reader knows something the characters don't; it could be scary!

**editing** – removing all unnecessary words from your story and getting it into the best shape possible

**editor** – the person who works in a publishing house and finds new books to publish. They also advise authors on how to improve their story by marking up words that need adding or removing

**first-person viewpoint** - a viewpoint that allows a single character to tell the story as if they had written it. The reader feels as if that character is talking directly to them, e.g. *It was July when I left for Timbuctoo. Just the thought of going back there made my heart sing.*

**foreshadowing** – dropping hints of coming events or dangers that are essential to the plot

**genre** – a particular type of fiction. 'Fantasy', 'historical', 'adventure' and 'science fiction' are all examples of different genres

**internal critic** – the voice that constantly picks holes in your work and makes you want to give up

**list** – the list of book titles that a publisher has already published or is about to publish

**manuscript** – your story when it is written down, either typed or by hand

**metaphor** – a way of describing something in a word picture. Calling a man 'a mouse' is a metaphor. It tells us that the man is timid or a coward, not that he actually *is* a mouse

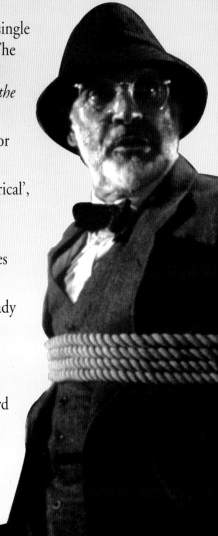

**motivation** – the reason why a character does something

**narrative** – the telling of the story or sometimes the story itself

**omniscient viewpoint** – an 'all-seeing' viewpoint that shows the reader the thoughts and feelings of all the characters

**plagiarism** – copying someone else's work and passing it off as your own. It is a serious offence

**plot** – the sequence of events that drives a story forwards; the problems that the hero must resolve

**point of view (POV)** – the eyes through which a story is told

**publisher** - a person or company who pays for an author's manuscript to be printed as a book and who distributes and sells that book

**sequel** – a story that carries an existing story forward

**simile** – describing something by saying it is *like* something else, e.g. 'clouds like frayed lace'

**synopsis** – a short summary that describes what a story is about and introduces the main characters

**theme** – the main idea behind your story, e.g. overcoming a weakness, the importance of friendship or good versus evil. A story can have more than one theme

**third-person viewpoint** – a viewpoint that describes the events of the story through a single character's eyes, e.g. 'Jem's heart leapt in his throat. He'd been dreading this moment for months.'

**unsolicited submission** – a manuscript that is sent to a publisher without them asking for it

**writer's block** – when writers think they can no longer write, or have used up all their ideas

Most well-known writers have their own websites. They will give you lots of information about their own books and many will give you hints and advice about writing too. Try David Almond's website at www.davidalmond.com

The *Listen and Write* pages on the BBC website are all about writing poetry, but there are lots of fun exercises with rap, similes and freeform verse that will make all your written words sparkle: www.bbc.co.uk/education/listenandwrite

Ask for a subscription to magazines such as *Cricket* and *Cicada* for your birthday. They publish the very best in young people's short fiction and you can learn your craft and read great stories at the same time. *Cicada* also accepts submissions from its subscribers. See both magazines at www.cricketmag.com

Make a good friend of your local librarian. They can direct you to useful sources of information that you might not have thought of. They will also know of any published authors scheduled to speak in your area.

Get your teacher to invite a favourite author to speak at your school.

## Places to submit your adventure fiction

• The magazine *Stone Soup* accepts stories and artwork from 8- to 13-year-olds. Their website is www.stonesoup.com

• The Young Writers Club is an Internet-based club where you can post your adventure-fiction stories. Check it out at: www.cs.bilkent.edu.tr/~david/derya/ywc.html

• *Potluck Children's Literary Magazine*: www.members.aol.com/potluckmagazine

• There are similar sites at www.kidauthors.com for 6- to18-year-olds.

• www.kidpub.org/kidpub is a subscription club that posts 40,000 young people's stories from all over the planet.

**Writing links** at Kids on the Net: www.kotn.ntu.ac.uk/creative/links.html and Google's Young Writers' Resource Directory: www.directory.google.com/Top/Arts/Writers_Resources/Young_Writers

## Adventure Books quoted or referred to in the text:

*The Wolves Chronicles,*
Joan Aiken, Red Fox 2000

*Kit's Wilderness, Skellig,*
David Almond, Hodder Children's Books 1999

*Lionboy,*
Zizou Corder, Puffin 2003

*The Great Elephant Chase,*
Gillian Cross, Puffin 1994

*The Wanderer,*
Sharon Creech,
Macmillan Children's Books 2001

*Sea Running,*
Tish Farrell, Macmillan Pacesetter 2000

*Two Weeks With The Queen,*
Morris Gleitzman, Puffin 1999

*Hoot,*
Carl Hiaasen, Macmillan 2002

*King Solomon's Mines,*
H. Rider Haggard, Thames Publishing Co

*Stormbreaker,*
Anthony Horowitz,
Walker Books 2004

*Kim,*
Rudyard Kipling, Macmillan 1949

*White Fang,*
Jack London, Parragon 1994

*The Kite Rider,*
Geraldine McCaughrean, Oxford University
P… 2001

*Kensuke's Kingdom,*
Michael Morpurgo, Mammoth 1999

*The Firework-Maker's Daughter,*
Philip Pullman, Corgi Yearling 1996

*Pirates!,*
Celia Rees, Bloomsbury 2003

*Treasure Island,*
Robert Louis Stevenson, Puffin Books 1994

*The Adventures of Huckleberry Finn,*
Mark Twain, Parragon 1994

*The Call of the Wild,*
Jack London, New Windmill, 1950

*The Tiger Rising*
Kate DiCamillo, Walker Books Ltd 1993

**A**

asking questions 17

audience finding 56–57

**B**

beginnings 23, 36–37

brainstorming 10–11, 13, 16, 17

**C**

characters 24–29, 37, 52

'classics' 34

climaxes 40

computer games 19

cover design 30, 55

criticism 51

**D**

dialogue 44–49

**E**

eavesdropping 46

editing 54, 60

endings 40–41

**F**

finishing touches 54–57, 58–59

**G**

getting started 8–13

glossary 60–61

**H**

heroes 24–29

**I**

ideas 14–23

imagery 42–43

impact 20–21

**J**

journals (diaries) 53

**L**

landscapes 20–23

locations 18–19

**M**

middles 38–39

motives 26

**N**

novels or short stories? 34–35

**O**

openings 23, 36–37

**P**

places to write 8–9

plots 32–41

points of view 30–31, 47, 61

primary sources 18–19

publishers 55, 56–57, 61, 62

**R**

reading habit 12–13, 57

regional accents 49

rewarding yourself 11

**S**

sequels 58–59, 61

settings 20–23

short stories or novels? 34–35

sources 18–19

speech 44–49

starting 8–13

story maps 33

styles 14–23

synopses 32–41, 61

**T**

titles 54–55

training 10

**V**

viewpoints 30–31, 47, 61

villains 26, 27

**W**

weaknesses 39

writer's block 50–53, 61

writer's experiences 6–7

writer's voice 14–15

writing materials 8

Picture Credits: Alamy: 14-15 all. Bridgeman Art Library: 13t, 24 all, 35tr, 36-37c, 38-39c. Corbis RF: 3, 4-5 all, 22b, 27 all, 28t, 29b, 34 all, 35b, 39r, 40l, 40-41b, 42-43b, 43t, 44-45 all, 46-47 all, 52-53c, 54t, 56-57 all, 62t. Creatas: 6-7 all, 8-9 all, 13b, 16-17 all, 18-19b, 19c, 22-23c, 37tr, 48t, 49t, 50t, 50-51c, 51r, 52t, 63br. FLPA: 10l, 18t, 19t, 20-21 all, 26-27c, 28l, 29c, 30b, 50-51b, 52b. Fotosearch: 28t, 58-59 all. Rex Features: 10t, 10-11c, 11r, 12, 22t, 25 all, 26t, 28-29c, 32-33 all, 42t, 48-49b, 54b, 55 all, 60-61c.